D1468632

MY FIRST PRAYER BOOK

MY FIRST PRAYER BOOK

TEXT BY
Frances Heerey, S.C.H.

ILLUSTRATIONS BY
Rita Goodwill

COVER ILLUSTRATION BY
George J. Angelini

THE REGINA PRESS
NEW YORK

Imprimatur:

C. Eykens, Vic. gen.
Antverpiae, 6 junii 1986

THE REGINA PRESS
145 SHERWOOD AVENUE
FARMINGDALE, N.Y. 11735

Copyright © 1986 THE REGINA PRESS

ISBN: 0-88271-131-8

All rights reserved. No part of this book may be reproduced in any form without permission in writing from the publisher.

Book design and typography by Roth Advertising.

PRINTED IN BELGIUM

TABLE OF CONTENTS

GENERAL PRAYERS

Jesus, when I opened my eyes this morning and saw the sun shining, I hopped out of bed, ran to the window, and said,

"Alleluia. Thank you, God for your gift of life today."

Why do I pray to You, my God?
Why do I want you near?
I know it's because you're my very best
     friend
And I enjoy each sound that I hear.
You speak in my heart so often
I shut my eyes real tight.
Your words stay long with me, God my
     friend
I know in my mind all is right!
I thank you for being my friend, my God.
And for loving me as you do.
I cannot tell you how happy I am
For having a friend like You.

Jesus, sometimes I lie in bed, my eyes wide opened in the dark, and I think of how near You are to me. I know I am not afraid of anything. Thank you for loving me.

Jesus, today is the first day of school. I am all excited. Give me a real good teacher, my old friends, and some new friends, too. Oh, and Jesus, help me with my school work, please, Thank you. Amen. Alleluia.

Jesus, sometimes I see people who are hurt. Sometimes they cry. Help me always to be kind and helpful to people who are hurting. Amen.

LOVE

God is love and I love God!
When I love You, God, I am happy.
When I love other people, I am happy.
Thank you, God, for helping me to love
and to be happy.

FAITH

I believe in You, God, I believe that in you
 are Three Divine Persons, the Father,
     the Son, the Holy Spirit.
I believe in your great love for me!
I believe all that you teach me about
     yourself,
I have faith in You, my God and my all.

HOPE

Hoping in You, my God, is believing that
     all good things will come my way,
     as you wish them to come.
I hope that one day I will be united
     with you forever and ever. Amen.

MORNING AND EVENING PRAYERS

When you wake up in the morning, kneel down and make the Sign of the Cross. Say the Our Father, the Hail Mary, the Glory Be, and the Apostles' Creed. These prayers can be found on page 31.

Here are some short prayers which take only a few moments to say.

A MORNING OFFERING

O Sacred Heart of Jesus,
I offer you this day
all my thoughts, words,
desires, and actions. Help
      me do
everything for you.

THE GUARDIAN ANGEL PRAYER

Angel of God, my guardian dear,
To whom His love commits me here,
Ever this day be at my side
To light and guard, to rule
      and guide.   Amen.

God, I believe all the truths
which you have taught us.

God, I hope for your grace on earth
and for eternal life with you in
heaven.

God, I love you with all my heart
and soul.

God, I am sorry for all my sins. Help
me never to commit them any more.

O sweetest Heart of Jesus,
I implore that I may ever love you
more and more.

Mary, you are my loving mother.
Keep me near you and your dear son,
Jesus, today.

Saint Joseph, watch over me today
just as you protected and cared
for the Child Jesus.

EVENING PRAYERS

Before you go to bed, kneel down and make the Sign of the Cross. Say the Our Father, the Hail Mary, and the Glory Be.
Here are some short prayers which take a few moments to say.

I adore You, God, I belong entirely
to you. I kneel in your presence and
adore You, my Lord and my God.

I thank you, God for keeping me
safe all day. Watch over me tonight.
All that I have and all that I am,
I have received from you.

I believe that you are here, God.
I lay myself down to rest in Your sight.

I hope, God, that you will protect
me always, day and night, and will
bring me safely through the years
of this life to the dawn of eternity.

I love you, God. You are all good
and I shall never stop loving You.
Teach me to love you more each day.

Mother Mary, pray for me to Jesus
who so often went to sleep
in your arms.

Saint Joseph, who watched over
the Child Jesus,
keep watch over me this night.

My Guardian Angel, remain by my side
every hour of the day and night.

Jesus, bless my father and mother,
and all those whom I love.

*(You may give the names of others
you wish God specially to bless.)*

Jesus, have mercy on the poor souls
in purgatory. Help them come to You.

PRAYERS TO JESUS

SOUL OF CHRIST

Soul of Christ, sanctify me.
Body of Christ, save me.
Blood of Christ, inebriate me.
Water from the side of Christ,
wash me.

Passion of Christ, strengthen me.
O good Jesus, hear me.
Within Your wounds, hide me.

Separated from you,
let me never be.
From the malignant enemy,
defend me.

At the hour of death, call me.
To come to You, bid me,
that I may praise You
in the company of Your saints,
for all eternity. Amen.

Jesus, I believe in You.
I believe you are the Son of God.
I believe You are God.
I believe You love me.
I hope in You. I love you, Jesus.

Jesus, I am sorry for anything
I did to hurt you or other people.
I promise that I will try to be kind
and loving. I love you.

Jesus, I want to ask you to bless
    my family
and my friends, but especially
those who have no one
to pray for them.

Jesus, I believe in You,
I hope in You, I love You
above all things.

Jesus, see how little I am
and how much I need to grow.
Make my soul beautiful
so that you will stay
with me always.

PRAYERS TO MARY

When I think of You, Mary, I get all glowing
inside. You are God's Mother and You
are my heavenly Mother. Always I want
to be pure like You, and kind like you.
Help me to love Your Son Jesus in a very
special way all my life. Amen.

THE MEMORARE

Remember,
O most gracious Virgin Mary,
that never was it known
that anyone who fled to your protection,
implored your help or sought your
intercession was left unaided.
Inspired with this confidence, I fly to you,
O Virgin of virgins, My Mother.
To you I come, before you I stand,
sinful and sorrowful.
O Mother of the Word Incarnate,
do not ignore my petitions,
but in your mercy
hear and answer me. Amen.

HAIL, HOLY QUEEN

Hail, holy Queen,
Mother of mercy!
Hail, our life,
our sweetness and hope!
To you do we cry,
poor banished children of Eve;
to you do we send up our sighs,
mourning and weeping
in this valley of tears!
Turn then, most gracious advocate,
your eyes of mercy toward us;
and after this, our exile,
show unto us the blessed
fruit of your womb, Jesus.
O clement, O loving,
O sweet Virgin Mary.

THE MAGNIFICAT

My soul proclaims
the greatness of the Lord
and my spirit exults in God
my Savior, because He
has looked upon
His lowly handmaid.

Yes, from this day forward
all generations will call me blessed,
for the Almighty
has done great things for me,
holy is His Name;
and His mercy reaches
from age to age
for those who fear Him.

He has shown the power
of His arm, He has routed
the proud of heart.
He has pulled down princes
from their thrones
and exalted the lowly.
The hungry He has filled
with good things, while the rich
He has sent away empty.

He has come to the help
of Israel His servant,
mindful of His mercy—
according to the promise He made
to our ancestors—of his mercy
to Abraham and his descendants
forever.

PRAYERS TO ST. JOSEPH

Dear St. Joseph. You were a wonderful father to Jesus. You worked hard. You were proud of your work as a father. You were a very good carpenter. Help me to take pride in the work I do each day. Amen.

Saint Joseph,
you loved the child Jesus with all your
heart.
Pray for me, a child who needs your love.

Help me Saint Joseph in my earthly strife,
ever to lead a pure and blameless life.

Saint Joseph,
please take care of me always,
now, and all through my life,
and especially when I come to die.

I want to follow your example,
Saint Joseph,
and love Jesus and Mary as you did.
Good Saint Joseph pray for me.

PRAYERS TO BE LEARNED BY HEART

THE SIGN OF THE CROSS

In the name of the Father,
and of the Son,
and of the Holy Spirit. Amen.

GLORY BE

Glory be to the Father
and to the Son
and to the Holy Spirit,
as it was in the beginning,
is now and ever shall be,
world without end. Amen.

GRACE BEFORE MEALS

Bless us, O Lord, and these Your gifts
which we are about to receive
from Your bounty
Through Christ our Lord. Amen.

GRACE AFTER MEALS

We give You thanks, O almighty God,
for all Your benefits;
You who live and reign,
world without end. Amen.

THE OUR FATHER

Our Father, who art in heaven,
hallowed be Thy name,
Thy kingdom come,
Thy will be done,
on earth as it is in heaven.
Give us this day our daily bread,
and forgive us our trespasses
as we forgive those
who trespass against us,
and lead us not into temptation,
but deliver us from evil. Amen

THE HAIL MARY

Hail Mary, full of grace,
the Lord is with thee;
blessed art thou among women,
and blessed is the fruit
of thy womb, Jesus.
Holy Mary, Mother of God,
pray for us sinners now
and at the hour of our death. Amen.

THE APOSTLES' CREED

I believe in God,
the Father almighty
creator of heaven and earth.
I believe in Jesus Christ, his only Son,
our Lord. He was conceived
by the power of the Holy Spirit
and born of the Virgin Mary.
He suffered under Pontius Pilate,
was crucified, died, and was buried.
He descended to the dead.
On the third day he rose again.
He ascended into heaven,
and is seated at the right hand
of the Father.
He will come again
to judge the living and the dead.
I believe in the Holy Spirit,
the holy Catholic Church,
the communion of saints,
the forgiveness of sins,
the resurrection of the body,
and the life everlasting. Amen.

ACT OF FAITH

O my God, I believe that you are
one God in three Divine Persons:
Father, Son and Holy Spirit.
I believe that Your Divine Son
became Man and died for our sins,
and that He will come again to
judge the living and the dead.
I believe these and all the truths
that the Catholic Church teaches,
because You have revealed them,
who can neither deceive nor
be deceived. Amen.

ACT OF HOPE

O my God, relying on Your
almighty power and infinite mercy
and promises, I hope to obtain
pardon of my sins, the help
of Your grace and life everlasting
through the merits of Jesus Christ,
my Lord and Redeemer. Amen.

ACT OF LOVE

O my God, I love You above all things
with my whole heart and soul,
because You are all good
and worthy of all love.
I love my neighbor as myself
for the love of You.
I forgive all who have injured me
and ask pardon of all
whom I have injured. Amen

PRAYER BEFORE A CRUCIFIX

Look down upon me,
good and gentle Jesus,
while before Your face
I humbly kneel and with burning
soul pray and beseech You
to fix deep in my heart
lively sentiments of faith,
hope and charity,
true contrition for my sins,
and a firm purpose of amendment.

While I contemplate,
with great love and tender pity,
Your five most precious wounds,
pondering over them within me
and calling to mind the words
which David, Your prophet,
said of You, my Jesus:

''They have pierced my hands
and my feet, they have injured
all my bones.'' Amen.

THE ROSARY

The rosary is a special way of praying to God that honors Mary, the Mother of Jesus. While reciting prayers, you think about certain stories in the lives of Jesus and Mary. These stories are called mysteries: a mystery is a story about God.

Rosary beads are used to keep count of the prayers and mysteries. Recite the Apostles' Creed while you hold the crucifix, then one Our Father and three Hail Marys. After that, as you think about each mystery, recite the Our Father on the large bead, the Hail Mary on each of ten smaller beads and finish with a Glory Be. That makes one decade. The complete rosary consists of five decades There are three sets of mysteries and five stories in each set.

THE JOYFUL MYSTERIES

1. The Coming of Jesus is Announced
2. Mary Visits Elizabeth
3. Jesus is Born
4. Jesus is Presented to God
5. Jesus is Found in the Temple

THE SORROWFUL MYSTERIES

1. Jesus' Agony in the Garden
2. Jesus is Whipped
3. Jesus is Crowned with Thorns
4. Jesus Carries His Cross
5. Jesus Dies on the Cross

THE GLORIOUS MYSTERIES

1. Jesus Rises from His Tomb
2. Jesus Ascends to Heaven
3. The Holy Spirit Descends
4. Mary is Assumed into Heaven
5. Mary is Crowned in Heaven

43

STATIONS OF THE CROSS

This is a prayer said during Lent. Many people say it all year round. There are fourteen stations.

Prayer
Jesus, I want to be sorry for my sins. Help me to see how you suffered and died for me. Help me to know your mercy and forgiveness. Teach me how to say ''Thank You.''

1. JESUS IS CONDEMNED TO DIE
   I am sorry, Jesus.

2. JESUS CARRIES HIS CROSS
   It looks so heavy, Jesus.

3. JESUS FALLS THE FIRST TIME
   Your strength is starting to fail.

4. JESUS MEETS HIS MOTHER MARY

How sad your Mother felt, Jesus.

5. SIMON HELPS JESUS

I must help others who carry heavy loads.

6. VERONICA WIPES JESUS' FACE

Teach me to help other in need.

7. JESUS FALLS A SECOND TIME

Dear Jesus, how weak you are.

8. JESUS MEETS THE WOMEN

Jesus you're so brave.
You tell them not to cry.

9. JESUS FALLS THE THIRD TIME

Dear Jesus, you are suffering so much.

10. JESUS IS STRIPPED OF HIS CLOTHES

How shamefully you were treated.

11. JESUS IS NAILED TO THE CROSS

How cruel the people were. I love you.

12. JESUS DIES

I know you forgive me my sins.

13. JESUS IS TAKEN DOWN

I thank the people who took care of your body.

14. JESUS IS LAID IN THE TOMB

Thank you for your mercy.

Come, O Holy Spirit, fill the hearts
of your faithful and kindle in them
the fire of Your love.

V. Send forth Your Spirit
and they shall be created.

R. And You shall renew the face
of the earth.

Let us pray;
O God, who has taught the hearts
of the faithful by the light
of the Holy Spirit,
grant that in the same Spirit,
we may be always truly wise
and ever rejoice
in His consolation.
Through Christ our Lord. Amen.

PRINTED IN BELGIUM BY
proost
INTERNATIONAL BOOK PRODUCTION